100 WINNERS
HORSES TO FOLLOW 2017

55th year of publication and
a companion volume to
100 Winners: Jumpers to Follow

GW00458737

Published in 2017 by Raceform Ltd
27 Kingfisher Court, Hambridge Road, Newbury, RG14 5SJ

A catalogue record for this book is available from the British Library.

ISBN 978-1-910497-18-0

Printed and bound in Great Britain by Keeps Printing, Newbury

100 WINNERS
Horses To Follow – Flat 2017

AKIHIRO (JPN)
3 b c Deep Impact – Baahama (Anabaa)
Unbeaten in two outings as a juvenile and with a
Group 3 already under his belt, this potentially top-
class son of Japanese super-sire Deep Impact is a
very exciting prospect for 2017. Master trainer Andre
Fabre will plot a campaign around the Derbys, with
Epsom a real possibility in June, and he ought to
have no trouble stepping up to 1m4f when you
consider his breeding. A sound surface suits and his
3yo return in a Classic trial is eagerly anticipated.
ANDRE FABRE

ALGOMETER
4 gr c Archipenko – Albanova (Alzao)
Algometer featured in this book last year and,
despite an abbreviated season, he managed to win
two of his five races and finish second in another.
His wins were at Listed and Group 3 level, but the
impression is that he can win at an even higher
grade this year. His two unplaced efforts were both
in Group 1s, the first in the Derby when he was
ridden more conservatively than usual (he was
absent for two and a half months afterwards), and
on his last start in Germany when the ground was
pretty soft and he reportedly "ran flat". Both those
races were over 1m4f, and it seems likely that a
similar trip to that will be in his favour this season,
as his dam excelled at the distance as a four and
five-year-old. His shrewd trainer can be expected
to find decent opportunities for him this season.
DAVID SIMCOCK

ALMANZOR (FR)
4 b c Wootton Bassett – Darkova (Maria's Mon)
Last season proved a revelation for the imperious
Almanzor, who held all before him after taking
the Prix Du Jockey Club at Chantilly, culminating
in success in the Champion Stakes at Ascot on
Champions Day. Jean–Claude Rouget, who himself
had a stellar year in 2016, resisted the temptation to
run in the Arc, reasoning that his top-class colt was
a 1m2f performer. However, as a 4yo it wouldn't at
all surprise were that to prove his ultimate goal as he
does have plenty of stamina on his dam's side. There
should be plenty of fun to be had with him again
along the way. JEAN–CLAUDE ROUGET

ALPHA DELPHINI
6 b g Captain Gerrard – Easy To Imagine (Cozzene)
Bryan Smart has an enviable record with sprinters
and he enjoyed Group 1 glory with this horse's half-
brother Tangerine Trees in 2011. Like him, Alpha
Delphini improved with age and last year, as a 5yo, he
was better than ever. Taking a handicap on his return
to action at Musselburgh in April from a mark of just
79, he defied a 4lb higher mark at York in July. Raised
another 5lb, he then edged out Final Venture at Ascot
two weeks later. At Beverley in August he took the
Listed Beverley Bullet in ultra–game fashion from
Willytheconqueror. On his final start in September
he confirmed himself a Group performer, despite
failing by a short head to take a Group 3 at Newbury.
A resolute battler, he is an out-and-out 5f performer
and capable of further improvement at six. There
are surely more good prizes coming his way. BRYAN
SMART

AL WUKAIR (IRE)
3 b c Dream Ahead - Macheera (Machiavellian)
By his own high standards Andre Fabre had a quiet

season in 2016 so he'll be hoping for much better this coming year. There are a few names of his to watch out for but one of the most exciting could be Al Wukair. A 200,000gns purchase in 2015, he made a successful racecourse debut in September in a 7f Saint-Cloud maiden, form that hasn't proved strong at the time of writing, but he really announced himself as a potential Group performer with an impressive display in Listed company at Deauville the following month. A colt with plenty of size about him, he's quoted at 33/1 for our 2000 Guineas but it remains to be seen whether he comes to Newmarket or stays in France for their big contests. ANDRE FABRE

ANDOK (IRE)
3 b c Elzaam – My Causeway Dream (Giant's Causeway)
Off the mark at the first time of asking in a 7f maiden at Redcar in July, this £60,000 Breeze-Up purchase followed up on his nursery debut at Doncaster in September from a mark of 80. Raised 5lb and sent back to the Town Moor the following month, he met traffic problems before finishing runner-up to another progressive type in Masham Star. Raced only over 7f so far, he will relish a slight step up in trip and hopefully will play his part in putting Richard Fahey past the 200 winners mark in 2017 after he fell just one short last time round. RICHARD FAHEY

ANEEN (IRE)
3 b f Lawman - Asheerah (Shamardal)
Having a well-known sibling can sometimes be a burden to connections, but thankfully those involved with Aneen know all about her half-brother and Irish 2000 Guineas winner Awtaad. As she is a filly, an attempt at that Classic is unlikely but she is sure to have her chance in Pattern class following a good

start to her career as a 2yo. She wasn't overly fancied on her debut over 7f when sent off at 5/1, but she caught the eye and made no mistake on her only other outing at the Curragh over the same distance. It will be interesting to see where she starts her 3yo campaign, but one would imagine she'll have a go in Group company sooner rather than later. KEVIN PRENDERGAST

ATTY PERSSE (IRE)
3 b c Frankel – Dorcas Lane (Norse Dancer)

The first member of Frankel's debut crop to appear in this book, Atty Persse made a winning start to his career in a maiden over a mile at Sandown. Pulling clear with next-time-out winner Hamada inside the final two furlongs, he took time to get organised but ultimately won with authority. He was soon purchased by Godolphin, who also owned the runner-up. This season, given his pedigree – his dam was a Listed winner over ten furlongs and placed twice at Group level over twelve – and the style of that success, he should excel as he steps up to middle distances. ROGER CHARLTON

BEAN FEASA
3 b f Dubawi – Speirbhean (Danehill)

Bean Feasa came into her racecourse debut over 6f at Naas with the reputation and market support that a half-sister to Teofilo would warrant. Having quickened to the front 1½ furlongs out it looked as if she would justify favouritism until she was overhauled late-on by the subsequent Coventry third, Psychedelic Funk. Such was the promise shown that to feature so little in her next two maidens was disappointing, though there were legitimate excuses. Firstly, in a strong 7f heat including the likes of Rhododendron, she missed the kick and found trouble in running late, then she failed to stay the mile after pulling too hard. Considering her pedigree and the potential on show at Naas it is hard to believe we have seen the best of this Irish Oaks entry. With handicaps now an option as well, getting off the mark is hopefully just a matter of time. JIM BOLGER

BOYNTON (USA)
3 ch c More Than Ready – Baffled (Distorted Humor)

This powerful American-bred carried his head high as he cosily saw off a host of future winners over 6f at Goodwood on his first outing in June. Then, stepped up a furlong in the Group 2 Superlative Stakes at Newmarket a month later, he knuckled down to defeat the very smart War Decree. Despite sweating up beforehand, starting slowly and getting caught on the outside he still finished 3/4l to the good. A return to Goodwood for the Vintage Stakes saw that form reversed, though on this occasion he seemed less at ease with the track as he navigated a racecourse bend for the first time. He did finish strongly, however, and, assuming he matures, a mile will be well within his compass this season. CHARLIE APPLEBY

BRIAN THE SNAIL (IRE)
3 gr c Zebedee – Sweet Irish (Shamardal)

This £50,000 yearling purchase won both his starts at two and looks a fine prospect for valuable sprint handicaps at three. Readily accounting for an exposed 75-rated rival on his debut at Pontefract in September, he followed up on totally different ground in a novice event at Catterick the following month, storming clear to score by seven lengths. Raceform commented: 'There is no telling how far he can go and he looks an interesting prospect as a sprinter next season.' No doubt a valuable 6f handicap at York in June will be at the back of his trainer's mind. This colt has already shown that he can handle all types of ground. RICHARD FAHEY

BRITTANIC (IRE)
3 ch c Excelebration - Fountain Of Peace (Kris S)

Brittanic wasn't seen on the race track until really late into his 2yo career, mid-December to be exact at Newcastle on the AW. He wasn't overly fancied, drifting from 9/2 to 7/1, but as the saying goes, horses don't know their odds and he duly won in taking style, landing a race that is working out nicely. Stepped up in trip slightly, he was next seen at the same course in January, this time in a conditions event, and made a big impression, winning easily. He looked Group class that day so it'll be interesting to see where connections send him next and a Guineas trial could well be on the agenda. DAVID SIMCOCK

CHAPKA (FR)
3 bl f Exchange Rate – Cheriearch (Arch)

A potential Stakes filly, Chapka got her career off to a perfect start in a warm back-end maiden on Deauville's Polytrack surface, coming out best in a tight three-way finish over 1m1f. She's out of a Listed winner and very much in the right hands with top French trainer Jean–Claude Rouget. Stepping up for a tilt at the Prix de Diane at Chantilly in June should be on her agenda and she's one to keep firmly on side. JEAN–CLAUDE ROUGET

CHIPPING (IRE)
3 b c Dark Angel – Bean Uasal (Oasis Dream)

By the sire of Mecca's Angel, Chipping cost 90,000euros as a yearling. A warm order on his belated debut on Newcastle's Tapeta in October, he raced on the opposite side of the track to the first two when a highly respectable third. On his only subsequent start two weeks later, he made no mistake at Redcar, beating an exposed 67-rated rival going away. From a mark in the low 70's he will be an attractive proposition in handicap company when he resumes his career and Raceform noted 'He has the scope to progress.' MICHAEL DODS

CLIFFS OF MOHER (IRE)
3 b c Galileo – Wave (Dansili)
The first foal of the lightly raced 5f all-weather winner Wave, who is a half-sister to three other winners, this son of Galileo emulated his relatives by taking a 7f Leopardstown maiden at the end of October, beating a better-fancied stable companion, Orderofthegarter, by a wide margin. The figures suggest he is Listed level at least, and he could be of interest as a possible Guineas contender, although he is currently a fair way down the pecking order at Ballydoyle. However, his trainer is not averse to having several contenders in the big races if they are thought good enough, and this one is open to plenty of improvement, so could prove to be a surprise package. AIDAN O'BRIEN

COLIBRI (IRE)
3 b c Redoute's Choice – High Days (Hennessy)
Colibri showed progressive form in three outings as a 2yo, firstly demonstrating ability when fourth of 13 at Newbury on his second start, and the form of that race could hardly have worked out better with the second, fifth, sixth, seventh (twice) and eighth all winning soon afterwards. The colt held a Group 2 entry at that stage, but didn't take it up and instead went on to dispose of five rivals by upwards of 12 lengths in a Brighton maiden in September. His breeding suggests that he should get a mile at least as a 3yo and it would be no surprise to see him net a decent prize or two this season. HUGO PALMER

CORONET
3 gr f Dubawi – Approach (Darshaan)
This highly regarded filly won both her juvenile starts and is a leading Oaks contender. Having landed a

Leicester maiden on her debut, she then beat the boys in the 1m2f Listed Zetland Stakes at Newmarket – a particularly promising performance considering she got behind and still looked green. She's a half-sister to St Leger runner-up Midas Touch and will stay well, and after her Newmarket win John Gosden said the Musidora would be used as a stepping stone to the Oaks. JOHN GOSDEN

CRACKSMAN
3 b c Frankel – Rhadegunda (Pivotal)
It has been well documented how successful Frankel was as a sire in 2016 and this colt played his part by winning his only start, a mile maiden at Newmarket in October. Sent off 9/2 third-favourite in a ten-strong field, the colt showed a thoroughly professional attitude to make a winning debut and the form was given substance by the subsequent success of his stablemate Stradivarius, who finished well behind him in fourth. A half-brother to a couple of winners, including the Group 3 winner Fantastic Moon, from the family of the 1,000 Guineas winner On The House, he may get a bit further than a mile in due course and, although it would be hugely optimistic to suggest that his owner has another Golden Horn on his hands, this colt is certainly an intriguing prospect for 2017. JOHN GOSDEN

CRIMEAN TATAR (TUR)
4 b c Sea The Stars – Unity (Sadler's Wells)
This completely unexposed 4yo colt goes into 2017 unbeaten in two outings. He made a belated winning debut in style at Newmarket over 1m4f in July, gaining an RPR of 96 in the process, and was then roughed off until a Listed race at Kempton in November on Polytrack. He came through successfully despite inexperience and showed a neat turn of foot. Trainer Hugo Palmer is targeting a Cup campaign

this season – his dam is half-sister to talented stayer Mizzou – and there ought to be plenty of improvement yet. It would be a surprise if he didn't at least land a Group race. HUGO PALMER

CRYSTAL OCEAN
3 b c Sea The Stars – Crystal Star (Mark of Esteem)
Closely related to multiple 10-12f Group race winner Crystal Capella and a half-brother to Listed 10f winner Crystal Zvezda, as well as 12f Canadian Group 1 winner Hillstar, Crystal Ocean's future belongs over a mile-and-a-half. So, given his potential over further, his promising debut second behind Warrior's Spirit over 7f at Newbury points to a colt of high calibre. He resembles his sire in looks and demeanour, and, like Sea The Stars, he is bound to improve for the experience gained from his first steps on a racecourse. He may well turn into an even better four-year-old but this season offers plenty with a Derby campaign not beyond the realms of possibility. SIR MICHAEL STOUTE

DABYAH (IRE)
3 b f Sepoy – Samdaniya (Machiavellian)
From the same connections as last season's Nell Gwyn winner and French 1000 Guineas runner-up, Nathra, Dabyah had a very similar two-year-old campaign to her stablemate and has the talent to follow nearly the same path at three. Both made successful starts to their racing careers before improving to win the same Newbury Conditions stakes over 7f in facile fashion. Each then stepped up to a mile and finished placed in Group 1 company, Nathra at Newarket, Dabyah in the Prix Marcel Boussac at Chantilly behind Wuheida. With a Guineas trial surely on the agenda, this daughter of an exciting young sire can continue to compete at the top level. JOHN GOSDEN

DANCE KING
7 ch g Danehill Dancer – One So Wonderful (Nashwan)

He is perhaps one of the more exposed runners in this book, but Dance King was better than ever at times last year and will resume from a mark he certainly can win off. He was tenth of 20 in a Doncaster Class 3 on his final outing of 2016, but didn't get much of a run following his customary sluggish start and finished with plenty of running left in him. Dance King will kick off from 4lb lower than when making a successful reappearance last May and should be placed to advantage. TIM EASTERBY

DHAJEEJ (IRE)
3 b c Cape Cross - Nimboo (Lemon Drop Kid)

Although Dhajeej didn't win as a 2yo, it seems unlikely that he'll remain without a victory for too long provided he doesn't significantly regress over the winter. His form figures won't appeal to some, with two seconds in his profile, but he didn't appear to do much wrong on both starts. His debut effort was promising in a race that, in all fairness, hasn't produced loads of winners but he didn't go backwards from that and at least matched that run when second again at Nottingham behind Tartini, a well-bred newcomer and another entrant in the 100, a contest that has seen a couple in behind successful since. A maiden or handicap can be taken with him before he creeps up in class. ROGER VARIAN

DOUBLE LADY (FR)
3 b f Stormy River – Montagne Magique (King's Best)

A useful maiden winner at Maisons-Laffitte on her second start, Double Lady was then sent off favourite for the Group 3 Oh So Sharp Stakes at Newmarket, which her trainer won with subsequent 1,000 Guineas winner Miss France in 2013. This filly managed only fifth, but the race did not set-up for her hold-up ride and she still impressed with how strongly she travelled. She could still be a Guineas contender. ANDRE FABRE

DREAMFIELD
3 b c Oasis Dream – Izzi Top (Pivotal)
Ultra-impressive when making a winning debut at Nottingham over 6f, this first foal of dual Group 1 winner Izzi Top had pretensions of making an impact over a mile, yet after a muddling test over Newmarket's 7f at the end of last season his trainer confirmed that sprinting would be his metier. The Pavilion Stakes at Haydock followed by the Commonwealth Cup at Royal Ascot is a soon-to-be well-worn path and, given how strongly he travels, they make desirable and ultimately winnable targets. Though sure to be highly competitive, few of his potential rivals would have left a visual impression as strong as Dreamfield, even if he does need to make a leap forward in form terms. JOHN GOSDEN

EARTHA KITT
3 b/br f Pivotal – Ceiling Kitty (Red Clubs)
Out of the stable's Queen Mary winner Ceiling Kitty, Eartha Kitt is certainly bred for the job and she could hardly have made a more promising debut in a 6f maiden at Haydock in September, being beaten just half a length into third behind Moonlit Show, a filly who went on to win a Listed race in Ireland on her next start. Eartha Kitt herself duly built on that initial effort when returned to the same C&D the following month, beating Cashla Bay, a John Gosden-trained filly who went on to win a Newmarket maiden on her next start. Although there is some stamina in her breeding, her pedigree is really all about speed and, currently rated 84, she could be just the type for some of those decent 3yo sprint handicaps once the turf season gets under way. TOM DASCOMBE

EASTON ANGEL (IRE)
4 gr f Dark Angel – Staceymac (Elnadim)
Sold for a Tattersalls February Sale record of
500,000gns, this former leading two-year-old
immediately picked up a brace of Listed races last
season before succumbing on the line to Prix De
L'Abbaye winner, Marsha when in search of the
hat–trick. Then, thrust into Group 2 company at
Goodwood, she was given plenty to do before finding
trouble-in-running again. It was another race that got
away, as she finished just half a length behind Take
Cover in fourth, and, remarkably, she is yet to win
at Group level. A no-show in the Nunthorpe, having
been impossibly drawn, should not take away from
the potential shown earlier in the season and it would
be surprising were she not to break her Group race
duck this year for new connections. MICHAEL DODS

ENABLE
3 b f Nathaniel – Concentric (Sadler's Wells)
With the future in mind Enable's debut success over a
mile, in what seemed an innocuous Newcastle maiden
at the end of November, was more than pleasing. The
turn-of-foot on offer points to a degree of potential
that will likely be fulfilled as she moves up to middle
distances. Subsequent winning exploits of the second
and fourth add further lustre to that performance.
She was allotted a mark of 84, which can surely be
exploited on the way to better things. JOHN GOSDEN

EVERYTHING FOR YOU (IRE)
3 b c Pivotal – Miss Delila (Malibu Moon)
A close relation of the same connections' Group 3
winner Ashadihan, Everything For You showed a
fair bit of ability on his debut in a Doncaster maiden
last year. He was never really going, yet kept on to
finish fourth of twelve and is open to bundles of
improvement. KEVIN RYAN

FAIR EVA
3 ch f Frankel – African Rose (Observatory)
Few fillies were subject to the level of hyperbole
reserved for this striking chestnut last season. Much
of it was merited following her demolition of Empress
and Sweet Solera Stakes winner, Nations Alexander
in a 6f Novice event at Haydock and the scorching of
the turf witnessed in Ascot's Listed Princess Margaret
Stakes. It appeared only injury or something special
could stop Khalid Abdullah's filly carrying all before
her. Instead, she put in two rather flat performances,
first behind Queen Kindly in the Group 2 Lowther
Stakes, where the 6f trip looked on the sharp
side and then in the 7f Group 2 Rockfel Stakes at
Newmarket, where again she appeared to lack a gear
possessed by the winner, Spain Burg. These suggest
pretensions of Guineas success were premature, yet
the spark characterising the first half of her two-year-
old campaign was notably absent in the second and
if that returns she will soon be right back in the mix.
ROGER CHARLTON

FAITHFUL CREEK (IRE)
5 b g Bushranger – Open Verse (Black Minnaloushe)
Mick Appleby, who does so well with second-hand
horses, paid 40,000gns for Faithful Creek out of Brian
Meehan's yard. This gelding has slipped right down
the ratings but did enough when seventh of 20 in the
Silver Cambridgeshire at Newmarket in September,
to suggest he's one to keep an eye on – that race went
the way of Mithqaal who has also done so well since
switching to Appleby's yard. He's had a handful of
outings on the all-weather for his new handler but
he should be even more interesting when returned to
handicaps on turf this year. MICHAEL APPLEBY

FINAL VENTURE
5 b g Equiano – Sharplaw Venture (Polar Falcon)
A winner of five races for Alan Swinbank, four of

them in 2016, Paul Midgley laid out 260,000gns to secure Final Venture at the Horses-in-Training Sale at Newmarket. On his final start for his previous handler, he finished fourth, beaten only about half-a-length in the Listed Beverley Bullet in August. Sent to Meydan in mid-January on his second outing for new connections, he defied a mark of 104 to take a valuable 6f handicap, making most of the running and winning by the minimum margin. All speed, he will play a part in the all the big sprint handicaps this year with further improvement still a possibility. PAUL MIDGLEY

FIRMAMENT
5 b g Cape Cross – Heaven Sent (Pivotal)
A move to David O'Meara's yard at the end of 2015 has brought about steady but significant improvement for Firmament, culminating in an admirable third in the Balmoral Handicap at Ascot when he was hampered in the final furlong. This was his third placed effort in a row at the same venue, the previous two displays coming over 7f, including an extraordinary mugging from an apparently rocket-fuelled Librisa Breeze. That gelding will have Group race aspirations this season and Firmament's shouldn't be any different, albeit over a mile. There is still scope to pick up a valuable handicap along the way, potentially at Royal Ascot, given the excuses available on Champions Day, but Listed and Group races will inevitably fill his schedule sooner rather than later. DAVID O'MEARA

FLEETFOOT JACK (IRE)
3 b c Kyllachy - Move (Observatory)
Fleetfoot Jack must have shown plenty of improvement between the two times he went through the sales ring, as he was sold for a fairly healthy 32,000gns in 2014 but that price sky-rocketed to 185,000gns just under a year later. His first two

starts were satisfactory performances but it was his
third run in a maiden that really caught the eye, a
keeping-on fourth at Redcar. He kicks off the season
on a mark of 67, which seems fair, and it would be
no surprise if he finishes it rated quite a bit higher,
as there is scope for him to improve when sent over
further than 7f. DAVID O'MEARA

FOREST RANGER (IRE)
3 b c Lawman – Alava (Anabaa)
A half-brother to the very useful Home Cummins,
who did these same connections proud, Forest Ranger
cost 26,000gns as a yearling and it already looks a
good buy. On his belated debut, he took a 7f maiden
at Redcar in September in comfortable fashion
and then finished a good third in the Listed Silver
Tankard over 1m at Pontefract in October. Raceform
reflected on his effort: 'He ran well given his lack of
experience and has the scope to do better at three.'
A likeable sort, he will stay beyond a mile and has
already shown he handles different goings. RICHARD
FAHEY

GALIKEO
3 b c Dansili – Galikova (Galileo)
This regally-bred colt was a talking horse last year in
France, but it wasn't until November that he made the
track, when narrowly failing to justify favouritism at
Deauville on Polytrack over 1m1f. Inexperience cost
him that day, but the ability was clear and it was a
decent maiden. He really ought to make the grade as a
3yo and the Prix Du Jockey Club at Chantilly in June
is his big initial target, before connections think about
taking on older horses later on. FREDDY HEAD

GARCIA
4 b g Paco Boy – Birdie (Alhaarth)
Having won three in a row, notably the Silver Bowl

at Haydock, Garcia's improvement had levelled out on his final start last year, when he was only fourth behind Morando at Ayr. However, he's had just six starts and should find further progress this term, especially when stepped up in distance from 1m. His dam won the 11.4f Listed Lingfield Oaks Trial.
RICHARD FAHEY

GIANT SPARK
5 b g Orientor – Annie Gee (Primo Valentino)
As his name might suggest, this sprinter has plenty of size and scope. Like his sire he is a late developer and in 2016 he improved a good deal to win four times in ten starts. Starting off at Redcar in May, he went in again at Nottingham in July and Thirsk in September. Having started the year rated just 62, he overcame a mark of 89 when scoring at Navan in October. Raceform had this to say: 'In really soft ground he could be up to contesting some Stakes sprints next season. He is a monster in size.' His trainer is good with these types of horses and, given suitable underfoot conditions, the gelding is likely to figure in the Ayr Gold Cup picture come September.
PAUL MIDGLEY

GLITTER GIRL
3 b f Invincible Spirit – Glitterball (Smart Strike)
This first foal of an unraced dam had her size, or rather lack thereof, continually referred to by her trainer last season and having had seven runs at two it may be questionable whether she has more to give at three. However, following a trio of taking wins last year she stepped into Pattern class and she performed with credit, each time leaving the impression that we had still not quite seen the best of her, particularly in the Rockfel Stakes behind Spain Burg at Newmarket. She even threatened to win that Group 2 before becoming unbalanced in the dip (eventually finishing

fourth) and it is realistic to imagine her winning at Listed level at least this year. WILLIAM HAGGAS

GOLD LUCK (FR)
3 b f Redoute's Choice – Born Gold (Blushing Groom)
As far as breeding goes, it's hard to find too many horses in training that match Gold Luck, as plenty of her relatives are at least Stakes-placed performers, and they include Goldikova, who won over £4,000,000 in prize money in her career. There is little chance that she'll come remotely close to that sort of level but she's already shown more than enough in two starts for Freddy Head to suggest she can win Pattern races. Her last run of 2016 saw her finish second in Listed company to another horse that features in this book, Al Wukair, and, while she was no match for that rival, there was plenty to like about the way she came home from the rear. She can only improve with age. FREDDY HEAD

HARRY ANGEL (IRE)
3 b c Dark Angel – Beatrix Potter (Cadeaux Genereux)
Following on from high-class Ribchester in 2015, Harry Angel became the second maiden in a row to land the Group 2 Mill Reef over 6f at Newbury in September. It was just his second outing, having narrowly failed in an Ascot maiden that May, but he was nevertheless sent off as favourite and later trainer Clive Cox admitted his home work had been out of the top drawer. Providing he matures from two to three, there's a strong chance he's a Group 1 winner in waiting and the Commonwealth Cup at Royal Ascot is the obvious target. CLIVE COX

HILARIO
3 b c Sepoy – Persario (Bishop Of Cashel)
A half-brother to Deacon Blues and The Tin Man, who both progressed with age to become high-class

sprinters, this is a promising colt. He won a Kempton maiden on his second start and then shaped better than the result when fifth in a Doncaster Listed race. That wasn't a strong contest, but he was unsuited by how it unfolded and he is open to plenty of improvement. CHARLES HILLS

HILARY J
4 b f Mount Nelson – The Terrier (Foxhound)
This filly was Ann Duffield's quickest juvenile but she suffered a fracture and didn't make the racecourse as a 2yo. After three placed efforts, she opened her account in a fillies' handicap in July at Thirsk from an opening mark of 70. Then, at Beverley the following month she defied a 4lb higher mark. Raised a further 7lb, she narrowly missed out when a close third at Nottingham in October. On her final start she finished an excellent fourth from a mark of 83 in a highly competitive 21-runner handicap at Doncaster. All speed, she can continue to make up for lost time at four. ANN DUFFIELD

HOLMESWOOD
3 b c Mayson – Anglezarke (Acclamation)
Holmeswood had just the two starts as a juvenile last autumn, both of them over 6f on Newcastle's Tapeta surface. Just touched off by a 92-rated rival in a five-runner maiden in October with the third horse miles behind, he had little difficulty in justifying odds-on in a bigger field at the same venue the following month. Very much bred for speed, it would be wrong to think that he is just an AW performer and, if that initial effort is taken at face value, his current mark of 84 could be lenient. It would be no surprise to see him do well in sprint handicaps when he does reappear. MICHAEL DODS

HORSEPLAY
3 b f Cape Cross – Mischief Making (Lemon Drop Kid

Horseplay must surely go down as one of the most visually stunning maiden winners in all of 2016. A nicely-bred daughter of Cape Cross, she made her debut at Ascot in a 7f contest on good to firm ground and her fourth place behind Kazimiera was a perfectly good start in a race that has worked out okay. However, after an 81-day absence and a switch to officially soft going (Raceform had it closer to good), she bounded away from her rivals over 1m down the home stretch at Nottingham, winning by 13 lengths. Since 2010, Andrew Balding has had five horses land a maiden by 10l or further, and they include Opera Gal (a three-time Listed winner) and Poet's Vanity (last year's Group 3 Oh So Sharp Stakes winner), so Horseplay has got every chance of being up to Pattern class. ANDREW BALDING

ICESPIRE
3 b f Frankel – Quest To Peak (Distant View)

Another 100 Winners entry sired by the mighty Frankel, Icespire was clearly expected to make a winning debut in a 7f fillies' maiden at Salisbury in October, but she still impressed with the way she scampered well clear of her rivals, recording a decent time in the process. Closely related to a French 1m4f winner and a half-sister to three other winners, including the top-class Special Duty, she is currently a top-price 40–1 for the 1,000 Guineas and is certainly worth her place in a trial should her connections send her to one. Her pedigree suggests she may get a bit further than a mile in due course and she is certainly an intriguing prospect. JOHN GOSDEN

INCONCEIVABLE (IRE)
3 b f Galileo – Mohican Princess (Shirley Heights

Inconceivable is a sister to three winners, including

100 Winners Horses to Follow Flat 2017

Group 3 winning stayer Eye Of The Storm, and
half-sister to a further five more including another
talented stayer, Curbyourenthusiasm. She had her
first look of a racecourse at Chelmsford over a mile
in a fillies' maiden where she made encouraging late
headway into fourth behind Elas Ruby. She should
improve with age and distance, which makes her a
three-year-old to follow, especially for a trainer who
has been so successful in the past with others of her
ilk. RALPH BECKETT

INTREPIDLY (USA)
3 b g Medaglia d'Oro – Trepidation (Seeking The Gold)
A $200,000 yearling, Intrepidly ran just twice at
two. After looking in need of the experience when
a staying-on fourth on his Yarmouth debut over 7f
in August (form which worked out well), he still
looked green on his second start over the same trip
at Kempton 55 days later, but he proved good enough
to see off his ten rivals in a time almost two seconds
quicker than the other division. It was perhaps no
surprise that he took to the synthetic surface so
well in view of his US pedigree, but he remains an
interesting prospect on any surface and on breeding
he should have little trouble in staying at least a mile
this season. JEREMY NOSEDA

JACK HOBBS
5 br h Halling – Swain's Gold (Swain)
Last season was certainly one to forget for Jack Hobbs.
Having sustained a stress fracture of his pelvis when
resuming at Newmarket in May, the 2015 Irish Derby
winner was forced onto the sidelines until making a
belated comeback in the Champion Stakes at Ascot
in October – a really hot event. John Gosden's team
produced him back to his best, however, and he ran a
really good race to finish third to Almanzor, the same

position he filled in 2015. Bred to get better as he gets older, this could be his big year and he should be up to adding to his Group 1 tally. JOHN GOSDEN

JOHANNES VERMEER (IRE)
4 b c Galileo – Inca Princess (Holy Roman Emperor)
The winner of the Group 1 Criterium International at Saint-Cloud in France as a two-year-old, Johannes Vermeer made only one appearance last year, when he turned up in a Newmarket Group 3 following an 11-month absence. He finished only third behind Muffri'Ha but shaped well. Aidan O'Brien said afterwards that was it for the season and that he was looking forward to racing the colt in 2017. AIDAN O'BRIEN

JOSHUA REYNOLDS
3 b c Nathaniel – Dash To The Front (Diktat)
A half-brother to dual 1m2f Group 1 winner Speedy Boarding, this colt did some good late work in a back-end Yarmouth maiden on his sole juvenile start and can develop into a nice sort over middle-distances this term. JOHN GOSDEN

KHAMAARY (IRE)
3 br f Tamayuz – Nufoos (Zafonic)
A half-sister to three smart winners including Awzaan, who won both the Mill Reef and Middle Park, this daughter of very useful racemare Nufoos won her sole start at two, a 6f maiden at Redcar in October. Showing her inexperience beforehand, she stayed on in willing fashion to get up near the line and score by a neck. She is obviously capable of much better at three. Raceform reported: 'She looks sure to improve significantly on this bare form.' MARK JOHNSTON

KHARBETATION (IRE)
4 b g Dream Ahead – Anna's Rock (Rock Of Gibraltar)

A half-brother to three winners, including Breton Rock, this rangy individual made £70,000 when going through the ring both as a foal and a yearling, but he has needed bags of time and had made just one racecourse appearance at the time of writing. At Thirsk in July he ran out a ready winner of a 1m maiden race but it was not all plain sailing. Difficult to load into the stalls, he missed the break and had to be pushed along in the early stages. Grasping the idea of things, he came back on the bridle turning in and stormed clear in the final two furlongs to hammer Ehtiraas, a highly-rated rival who won his next outing by 5l. He suffered a series of niggling problems afterwards and did not reappear. Connections think they have a Group performer on their hands in time, but first of all he will have to learn his trade in handicaps. DAVID O'MEARA

KITTEN'S JOHNSTOWN (USA)
3 ch c Kitten's Joy – Cellars Shiraz (Kissin Kris)

Bought for 85,000gns at the Breeze-Up sales, this American-bred colt is a half-brother to five winners and already looks a good purchase. Kevin Ryan had his usual successful season with 97 winners in 2016 including the Ayr Gold Cup with Brando. At the Western meeting the previous day he introduced Kitten's Johnstown, who made every yard to win in good style chased home by Trading Point, a next-time-out winner. Raceform reckoned: 'He looks a nice prospect and should get further'. In time he could prove very useful. KEVIN RYAN

KRUGER PARK (IRE)
3 br c Requinto – Definite Opinion (Kheleyf)

The much missed former jockey, award winning journalist, TV presenter and jockey coach Tom O'Ryan napped newcomer Kruger Park in a charity

tipping competition on the final day of the hugely
successful Yorkshire festival at Pontefract in July. A
£40,000 Breeze-Up purchase, he looked the part in
the paddock but was the only one without a start
in the six-strong field, and his inexperience told.
He kept on nicely in the closing stages to finish a
highly respectable fifth, prompting Raceform to add
'improve' to his in-running comment. That he did,
taking a maiden at York in September after travelling
strongly and only needing to be kept up to his work.
He will start life in handicaps from a mark in the low
80's, and hopefully will prove much better than that
by the end of his second season. RICHARD FAHEY

LEFT HAND
4 ch f Dubawi – Balladeuse (Singspiel)
Last season this filly really built on her fourth in the
Prix Marcel Boussac as a juvenile. After a staying on
fourth in the Prix Saint-Alary on her reappearance,
she chased home the brilliant La Cressoniere in the
Prix de Diane when a 50/1 outsider. She backed
that up by taking the Prix Psyche at Deauville before
gaining her first Group 1 success in the Prix Vermeille
on her first try at 1m4f. After that she took her
chance in the Prix de L'Arc de Triomphe, but was
drawn wide and never got involved. She kept the best
company last season, but did not have that much
racing and remains relatively unexposed at 1m4f. She
looks set to make her mark in the top fillies' races
at around that trip this season. CARLOS LAFFON–
PARIAS

LIBRISA BREEZE
5 gr g Mount Nelson – Bruxcalina (Linamix)
The 2016 season saw consistent improvement for
Librisa Breeze to the extent that he now looks a
Group 1 sprinter in the making. Since barely wanting
for stamina at the end of Ascot's straight mile in
the Royal Hunt Cup he has thrived. An emphatic

success in Ascot's International Stakes over a furlong
shorter followed, before the grey dipped his toe into
Group class waters at York, where he ran with credit
in fourth behind former stablemate Nemoralia. A
return to Ascot and handicap company then saw
him pull off one of last season's most extraordinary
performances. Settled in rear from the off, he found
himself behind a wall of horses as they entered the
final furlong. Once the gap appeared the race was all
but over, yet he produced a rare turn of foot to collar
Firmament and Squats. Such was the speed on show
that a return visit to Ascot in the Group 1 Champions
Sprint over 6f beckoned. Forced to make his move
on the unfavourable side of the track that day he
still made eye-catching headway into sixth. This year,
still unexposed at 6f, if he can utilise his acceleration
appropriately, races like the Diamond Jubilee and
Haydock Sprint Cup become appealing targets. DEAN
IVORY

LIMATO (IRE)

5 b g Tagula – Come April (Singspiel)

This gelding developed into a genuine Group 1
performer last season, competing at that level on all
his starts and winning twice, firstly the July Cup in
imperious fashion and then sweeping past his rivals
to win the Prix de la Foret at the Arc meeting, a race
in which he had been runner-up as a 3yo. His defeats
came when tried at distances other than six and seven
furlongs; he lost out to 5f specialist Mecca's Angel
in the Nunthorpe, and was fourth and sixth in the
Lockinge and Breeders' Cup Mile respectively. Those
latter runs are the only occasions he has finished out
of the first two, and even then he was not beaten far,
although looking less potent over the extra furlong.
He has not had that much racing for his age and,
given he will be fully mature this season, may be able
to manage that elusive 1m win in something like the
Sussex Stakes. However, provided he gets a sound

surface, he is sure to be a major player in the top 6f
and 7f races once more. HENRY CANDY

MAKE TIME (IRE)
3 ch c Makfi – Poppet's Lovein (Lomitas)
Make Time was sent off at 50/1 for his debut in a
fast-ground Ascot maiden over 7f last September,
but belied those odds by going down by just a nose.
He proved that initial effort was no fluke over the
same trip at Salisbury later in the month, ploughing
through the soft ground to bolt up by five lengths.
The form of that race received several boosts
subsequently and he was a possible for the Racing Post
Trophy at that stage, but ultimately he didn't go to
Doncaster. There is some stamina in his pedigree, so
he should have no problem in getting a mile and looks
an interesting prospect as a 3yo for his up-and-coming
trainer. DAVID MENUISIER

MAKKAAR (IRE)
3 b c Raven's Pass – Beneventa (Most Welcome)
A half-brother to three winners, including the smart
Bow Creek for the same stable, Makkaar changed
hands for 85,000gns as a yearling. After a good
effort when third of four on his debut at Beverley in
September, he followed that up with a placed effort
at Leicester. At Newmarket in October he put his
previous experience to good use, making every yard
and accounting for eight newcomers, going away at the
end. He will be ideally suited by a mile or further at
three and looks just the progressive type his record-
breaking trainer excels with. MARK JOHNSTON

MALMOOSA (IRE)
4 b f Shamardal – Mohafazaat (Sadler's Wells)
A big filly, Malmoosa came good in a Lingfield
handicap in August before progressing again to finish
second in a 1m2f fillies' handicap at Newmarket in

October. She was below form at Doncaster on her
final start of the campaign, but had probably had
enough by then and she could make the jump into
Pattern company this term. BRIAN MEEHAN

MONARCHS GLEN
3 b c Frankel - Mirabilis (Lear Fan)
Frankel was the sire everyone wanted to know
about last year and his 2yos did him proud without
securing a really big-race win. This season will also be
fascinating for his stock, as we get the chance to assess
whether some of his promising types train on as well
as he did. One such horse is Monarchs Glen. Not out
of a superstar mare, this colt ran both his races as
a juvenile over 1m1f at Goodwood, so he can't have
been showing a tonne of pace at home. His debut
promised plenty and he duly built on that to land
odds of 1/3 on similar ground 18 days later. It would
appear that middle-distances will be his optimum
starting point in 2017, almost certainly in handicaps.
JOHN GOSDEN

NATIONAL DEFENSE
3 b c Invincible Spirit – Angel Falls (Kingmambo)
A sibling to a pair of winning fillies, this colt
outstripped his relatives in just three starts as a
juvenile. He made all to bolt up in an ordinary
Deauville maiden for unraced colts in August, but
then proved one-paced when upped to a Group 3 next
time, when ridden more conservatively. However,
he put that run behind him when again making the
running in the Group 1 Prix Jean-Luc Lagardere at
the Arc meeting. Travelling strongly at the head of
affairs, he found plenty when asked to score by a wide
margin. He is related to a 1m4f winner, but, given his
style of racing, it seems likely that a mile will remain
his ideal trip in the short term. His trainer has often
brought her best colts and fillies to Newmarket in

May, but given the likely strength of the Coolmore battalions, he may well stay at home with the Poule D'Essai des Poulains his early season target before a tilt at the St James's Palace at Royal Ascot. If he progresses as expected, there are a number of good races to be won with him. CRIQUETTE HEAD–MAAREK

OMRAN
3 ch c Choisir – Ruff Shod (Storm Boot)
Omran wasn't seen until right at the end of 2016, but he soon made quite an impression. Narrowly beaten on his debut in a 6f Doncaster maiden on the very last day of the turf season, he was stepped up a furlong at Chelmsford the following month and easily disposed of his eight rivals by a wide margin. Although by a top-class sprinter, there is a good deal of stamina on the dam's side, with one of his siblings winning at up to 1m5f on the Flat and another successful at up to 3m1f over hurdles. He certainly seemed to appreciate the longer trip on his second start and we should be hearing plenty more of him as a 3yo, probably over middle distances. MARCO BOTTI

OUJA
3 b f Sea The Stars – Royale Danehill (Danehill)
Finishing tenth of 14 in a Doncaster maiden wasn't an obviously promising debut from Ouja, but it should be noted that she went off 13/8 favourite for a race her trainer has run some good horses in over the years. A 200,000gns daughter of Sea The Stars, we can expect to see a different filly this season. JOHN GOSDEN

PARLANCE (IRE)
3 b f Invincible Spirit – Pleasantry (Johannesburg)
Parlance ran three times at two and each of her performances was a big improvement on the previous one. A disappointing second-favourite on her debut

over 5f at Nottingham in June, she took a big step
forward when beaten a head over an extra furlong
at Kempton when reappearing nearly four months
later. She progressed again when stepped up to 7f
at Chelmsford the following month, making all and
winning easily. She cost 450,000gns as a yearling and
is related to the likes of Kingman and Oasis Dream on
the dam's side, so getting a win out of her would have
been important, but she can probably land something
rather better this year at up to a mile and there is no
reason to believe that she can't do it on grass as well.
SIR MICHAEL STOUTE

PEALER (GER)
3 b c Campanologist – Praia (Big Shuffle)
When Pealer made his racecourse debut at Goodwood
in October he wasn't expected to trouble his
stablemate Monarchs Glen judged on the betting, but
he really caught the eye with a staying-on second,
beaten 1¼ lengths. A 140,000gns purchase in 2015,
this son of Campanologist is bred to be well-above
average and is a half-brother to the really consistent
Group campaigner Potemkin, who won a 1m2f heavy-
ground Group 1 contest in November for Andreas
Wohler. One would imagine that he's going to be
most effective in middle-distance events, especially as
his sire was a multiple winner at 1m4f, four times at
Group 1 level. JOHN GOSDEN

POET'S WORD (IRE)
4 b c Poet's Voice – Whirly Bird (Nashwan)
Poet's Word was just a handicapper in 2016, but he
looks a potential Group 1 horse for a trainer who's a
master at getting horses to progress through the ranks.
Having won a Nottingham maiden that has worked
out really well, Poet's Word was only fourth when
favourite for an Epsom handicap on Derby day – a
race Sir Michael Stoute has a good record in. However,
he showed his true worth at Goodwood next time,

winning a hot race from an unpromising position. He was then only second to Central Square at Doncaster on his final outing of the campaign, but that still represented further progress and it's likely there's a lot more to come yet, especially when he's upped to 1m4f. SIR MICHAEL STOUTE

QEMAH (IRE)
4 b f Danehill Dancer – Kartica (Rainbow Quest)
Qemah was included in this book last season and did us proud, winning three of her five races, including the Group 1 Coronation Stakes and Prix Rothschild, as well as being placed in the others, making her one of the top fillies of her generation. So far she has raced mainly at a mile, a trip which suits her well, and she could well make her mark against the colts at that trip. However, her pedigree suggests she might stay 1m2f this season, which increases her options. Whatever route she takes, she is worth keeping onside. JEAN–CLAUDE ROUGET

QUIET REFLECTION
4 b f Showcasing – My Delirium (Haafhd)
The winner of three of her four starts at two, Quiet Reflection made giant strides in her second season. She won four of her first five starts and proved herself as one of the top spinters in Europe. Partnered by former jump-jockey Dougie Costello, she kicked off by taking a Group 3 at Chantilly in April. She was a clear-cut winner of the Group 2 Sandy Lane at Haydock the following month before going on to take the second running of the Group 1 Commonwealth Cup at Royal Ascot. On ground quicker than ideal she then finished a highly respectable third behind Limato in the July Cup. Back on her favoured easy ground she defeated the subsequent Champions Sprint winner The Tin Man and the July Cup runner-up Suedois in the Haydock Sprint Cup. On her final start she was below her best behind The Tin Man at Ascot,

finishing seventh of thirteen. Although she handles quickish ground, she is at her happiest when able to get her toe in. Ground conditions will determine where she will appear on her return to action with the Temple Stakes at Haydock and the Duke Of York high on the list before she returns to Royal Ascot for the Diamond Jubilee Stakes. She has done her syndicate owners proud with more big pay-days at the elite fixtures to come. KARL BURKE

REDICEAN
3 b c Medicean – Red Halo (Galileo)
Redicean will start his 2017 campaign from a mark of 85 but there's every reason to think he will prove to be much better than that. He was campaigned like a good horse last year, firstly when taken to Ascot for his debut, where he showed ability. He was turned over at odds-on at Wolverhampton next time, but Peter Chapple-Hyam then ran him in the Listed Zetland Stakes and the colt shaped okay, not getting the best of runs before his bid flattened out. It's worth noting he was entered in the Group 1 Racing Post Trophy, a race in which his trainer has a good record, and the suspicion is he will develop into a smart sort. PETER CHAPPLE–HYAM

REMARKABLE
4 b g Pivotal – Irresistible (Cadeaux Genereux)
Benefiting from the experience of one run at two and the application of blinkers, Remarkable started last season with a pair of successes; first at Southwell over 7f, and then at Doncaster in a 6f handicap where he left a lasting impression, flying home to beat Alqubbah. Listed class followed at Newbury, where he shaped comfortably like the second-best horse in a race stolen by Log Out Island, and then he more than justified his place in the Group 2 Jersey Stakes, finishing a good fifth behind Ribchester. Gelded soon after, he returned to Ascot and perhaps

ran like a horse who had been off the track for 108 days. Risking an extra furlong, connections opted to wrap up his season in the 1m Balmoral Handicap on Champions Day and, despite being ridden handier than usual, he handled it well. Yuften's waywardness in the final furlong forced him sideways but he was not going to improve upon second. This season he has the potential to compete at Pattern level and he has a plethora of options between 6f and a mile. JOHN GOSDEN

RIBCHESTER (IRE)
4 b c Iffraaj–Mujarah (Marju)

A smart juvenile who won the Mill Reef Stakes on his third and final start of 2015, this rangy colt became one of Europe's top milers at three. After he was second and then disqualified in France on his return, he justified his trainer's confidence in his ability when finishing an excellent third behind Galileo Gold in the 2,000 Guineas, outrunning odds of 33/1. After a clear-cut success in the Group 3 Jersey Stakes at Royal Ascot, he returned to Group 1 company, finishing third, beaten just a neck and a short head behind The Gurkha and Galileo Gold in the Sussex Stakes. At Deauville in August he captured the Prix Jacques Le Marois, beating the likes of Vadamos and Ervedya, before going down by under by half a length to the filly Minding in the Queen Elizabeth II Stakes. After a trip to Dubai in the spring it will be the Lockinge ahead of the Queen Anne at Royal Ascot, with all the Group 1 mile races sure to figure thereafter. RICHARD FAHEY

ROYAL ARTILLERY (USA)
4 b/br c War Front – Masseuse (Dynaformer)

An impressive maiden winner at Doncaster on his sole two-year-old start, Royal Artillery was beaten on his first couple of outings last term, but he confirmed that initial promise when coming good again in the

Group 3 Rose of Lancaster Stakes at Haydock – he outbattled Scottish, who won at the same level next time, before finishing runner-up in the Caulfield Cup. John Gosden's colt was turned out again quite quickly, just nine days later, in a Group 2 at Deauville in France, and he managed only third, but the winner was Almanzor, who had already won the French Derby and later landed the both the Irish and British Champion Stakes. This son of War Front is a big colt who still has improvement in him, so it bodes well that he's already at a smart level. JOHN GOSDEN

SACRED ACT
6 b g Oasis Dream – Stage Presence (Selkirk)
This six-year-old has stood little racing, just five starts – two in 2014, two in 2015 and only one last year. However, he has shown himself to be decent and with the potential for more, if he can stand further training. He won that sole outing last season, despite being really weak in the market and finding all the trouble going. He looks made for the Lincoln at Doncaster, so will hopefully appear among the entries. JOHN GOSDEN

SAINT EQUIANO
3 b c Equiano – St Athan (Authorized)
Former jockey Keith Dalgleish has made great strides up the training ranks and his final total of 81 winners in 2016 broke his own record for a Scottish-based handler. Well beaten in a novice event when sent off favourite on his debut at Carlisle in June, Saint Equiano showed what had been expected of him that day when finishing runner-up at Ayr's Western meeting in September. On his third and final start the following month, he opened his account on a return visit to the Scottish track, making every yard and shooting clear to score in fine style. Raceform commented: 'He looks a nice prospect.' Connections

have dabbled with a hood so he has his quirks but, clearly going the right way, he will stay at least a mile as a 3yo and looks sure to add to his tally when he dips his foot into handicap company. KEITH DALGLEISH

SCOONES
3 ch c Sepoy – Hannda (Dr Devious)

Despite not showing obvious promise on his only start so far on rain-softened ground over a mile at Nottingham, this colt is from a family whose members, including Group 1 winner Seal Of Approval, have been allowed to mature slowly by his same patient connections. Coupled with his exciting young stallion, who has already made an impact with his two-year-olds last season, there is every reason to expect a much improved showing this time around, with trips in excess of a mile expected to prove well within his compass. JAMES FANSHAWE

SENGA (USA)
3 b f Blame – Beta Leo (AP Indy)

Senga improved in each of her three outings as a juvenile but it was her final run which really marked her down as one to follow in 2017. Having turned over a hot-pot in a conditions event at Saint–Cloud, the daughter of US sire Blame was a huge eyecatcher when placed in the Prix Marcel Boussac on Arc day the following month. She stood no chance of winning, having been held up off a false pace but she ran on very promisingly all the same. Trainer Pascal Bary knows all about handling a top miler and she must be a player against her own sex this term. Ultimately the Breeders' Cup is an end-of-year aim. PASCAL BARY

SOFIA'S ROCK (FR)
3 b c Rock Of Gibraltar – Princess Sofia (Pennekamp)

A brother to three winners, Sofia's Rock cost

100,000euros as a yearling. In the frame at Redcar, Haydock and Hamilton on his first three starts, he broke his duck when returning from a two-month break over 1m1f at Redcar in October, making every yard to take the Double Trigger maiden by 7l. That is a race his trainer obviously targets because it's run in honour of his former champion stayer. Stamina is clearly his strong suit and he looks the sort of tough and determined galloper his trainer excels with.
MARK JOHNSTON

SO MI DAR
4 b f Dubawi – Dar Re Mi (Singspiel)
A daughter of the top-class mare Dar Re Mi, this filly has won four of her five races to date, and might have won more but for suffering a mid-season setback. After taking her sole start as a juvenile, she returned to beat colts in the Derby Trial at Epsom, despite her rider dropping his whip. She followed that up with an impressive victory in the Musidora Stakes, which marked her down as the main threat to Minding for the Oaks. However, she sustained an injury shortly afterwards which kept her off the track for the whole of the summer. She returned to defy a penalty in a fillies' Listed race at Yarmouth's big September meeting, which set her up nicely for a crack at the Prix de L'Opera, her first try at Group 1 level. Sent off at odds on, she did not get the best of runs and was unable to quite get to a pair of older fillies who had both previously won at the top level. Not seen again, she gives every indication that there is plenty more to come in 2017, and it should also be remembered that her dam did not win her first Group 1 until she was a four-year-old. Expect to see her contesting many of the top middle-distance fillies' races this coming season. JOHN GOSDEN

STARGAZER (IRE)
4 b c Canford Cliffs – Star Ruby (Rock Of Gibraltar)
Stargazer won a hot Sandown handicap on his
reappearance, then twice shaped well in defeat in
what was a light campaign. He was a close third,
having been caught wide, at Glorious Goodwood, and
then met significant trouble in running at Ascot. He's
had just six starts overall and is open to lots more
improvement. SIR MICHAEL STOUTE

STONE THE CROWS
3 b g Cape Cross - Stars In Your Eyes (Galileo)
Stone the Crows has a really nice pedigree so he can't
have been the easiest at home given that he's already
been gelded. His trainer didn't send him to the course
until November, but he showed plenty of promise in
a 1m Nottingham maiden, with the horse one place
behind him going on to score next time. He had one
more run, this time at Kempton, where he went
up in trip but found Azam, a colt trained by John
Gosden, 6l too good. That effort suggested he may
still want further, so, hopefully, with a maiden success
under his belt before too long, he can make up into
a nice middle-distance handicapper. His half-brother
Banksea finished 2016 officially rated 100. ROGER
CHARLTON

SWISS STORM
3 b c Frankel – Swiss Lake (Indian Ridge)
A son of Frankel and from a likeable, speedy family
on the dam's side, Swiss Storm was unplaced at
odds-on in a 6f Haydock maiden on his debut, but
he showed himself to be a useful prospect when
taking a 7f Newbury maiden next time, beating Sir
Michael Stoute's City Of Joy, a next-time-out winner.
A powerful-looking colt, he's probably going to reach a
smart level. DAVID ELSWORTH

TALAAYEB
3 b f Dansili – Rumoush (Rahy)

A Hamdan Al Maktoum filly who is out of a half-sister to the owner's 1,000 Guineas winner Ghanaati, Talaayeb impressed when making a winning debut in a 7f Newmarket maiden, picking up well after travelling easily. Trip-wise, it's hard to say whether she should be on the Guineas trail or is more of an Oaks type, and it's possible neither will be suitable and that she'll make more of 1m2f horse. But there's no doubt about her talent – she's good, and it will be interesting to see how her campaign unfolds. OWEN BURROWS

TARTINI (USA)
3 ch c Giant's Causeway – Vignette (Diesis)

From an eminently likeable family, this half-brother to winners including St Leger hero Lucarno and the talented stayer Flying Officer, was largely unconsidered when making a winning racecourse introduction at Nottingham in October. Green in the early stages, he made up significant ground under Robert Tart in the last two furlongs to beat the more experienced Dhajeej (another entrant in this publication) in decisive style. Stamina promises to be his forte and, given the hint of class on show here, it is easy to imagine a season geared around races like the Bahrain Trophy, Gordon Stakes and Great Voltigeur before an attempt to replicate his most illustrious sibling at Doncaster. JOHN GOSDEN

THE TIN MAN
5 b g Equiano – Persario (Bishop Of Cashel)

When he made the frame in the Champions Sprint Stakes on just his sixth career start at three in 2015, it was clear The Tin Man had a big future ahead. His 4yo campaign wasn't always plain sailing as he wasn't always right at home, but he still won three of his

five starts culminating in success back at Ascot in
the big one on Champions Day. He came of age that
day, proving he can knuckle down as well as glide
through his races, and there's still likely more to come
this season as his comeback will be just a 12th career
start. One would imagine that Ascot in October will
be his big aim again. JAMES FANSHAWE

TIGERWOLF (IRE)
4 br g Dream Ahead – Singing Field (Singspiel)
We've probably only seen glimpses of what this horse
could be capable of so far in eight career starts. He
was entered in last year's 2,000 Guineas, so has clearly
long been well regarded. So far he has just a Salisbury
maiden win to show for his efforts, and he made a
meal of that, but he's a big sort with plenty of raw
talent and could make good progress as he matures.
Three starts back, just prior to the maiden win,
Tiger Wolf would have won a competitive Goodwood
handicap had the race unfolded more kindly (he
was continually denied a run and went under by
less than a length). He was below form on his final
start of 2016 but will resume from 2lb lower than at
Goodwood. MICK CHANNON

TRADING POINT (FR)
3 b c Siyouni – Zita Blues (Zieten)
Bought for 100,000euros at a Breeze-Up Sales, Trading
Point, a half-brother to eight winners, finished
runner-up on his debut at Ayr's Western meeting in
September, chasing home a potentially very useful
sort in Kitten's Johnstown (another entrant in this
book). Sent to Haydock the following month, he took
a 1m maiden, forging clear before idling in the closing
stages. Likely to be suited by 1m2f plus at three,
he looks sure to make a useful handicapper. JOHN
QUINN

UAE KING

3 b c Frankel – Zomaradah (Deploy)

Expectations for this Frankel half-brother to Dubawi deserved to be sky high before his debut over a mile at Newbury in October and he was duly sent off the 7/2 joint favourite for that contest. Drawn on the stands-side rail, this solid colt travelled smoothly into the penultimate furlong before dropping away, crucially isolated from the main action in the centre of the track. Finishing seventh, 6¼l behind the winner Rosarno was no disgrace and he showed more than enough to suggest there is much better to come this term. Bred to excel over middle distances, he should win a maiden before raising his sights towards the level of those expectations. ROGER VARIAN

ULYSSES (IRE)

4 ch c Galileo – Light Shift (Kingmambo)

A son of Galileo, this colt created a good impression on his sole start as a juvenile in 2015 and was included in this publication last year as a result. He was narrowly beaten on his reappearance in a Leicester maiden, but that proved a good race, with the winner Imperial Aviator bolting up in the ultra-competitive London Gold Cup on his next outing, and the three that followed him home, all six lengths and more adrift, all scoring subsequently. With that run under his belt, he flew home in a 1m2f maiden at Newbury, leaving seven subsequent scorers well in his wake. That performance encouraged connections to let him contest the Derby, but the race probably came too soon in his career and he finished in the rear. He returned to action in the Group 3 Gordon Stakes at Goodwood and finished well to get the better of three Irish challengers. He was then dropped back to 1m2f, but, despite running arguably his best race to date, lost out to the progressive 4yo filly Chain Of Daisies by a narrow margin. It was slightly surprising that he was then sent to contest the Breeders' Cup Turf, but he ran with credit against older rivals, finishing fourth to the tough Group 1 competitors Highland Reel and Flintshire, with Arc winner Found in third. Those two tough races should have taught him a lot and, with his handler a master at training older colts, Ulysses can justify the esteem in which he is held this season. SIR MICHAEL STOUTE

VAZIRABAD (FR)
5 b/br g Manduro – Visorama (Linamix)
This French-bred gelding did us proud last year, winning four of his six races and being narrowly beaten in one of the others. He was arguably the best stayer in Europe, winning a second Group 1 Prix Royal-Oak, plus Group 2s in Dubai and France, and getting touched off in the Prix de Cadran on his first try at 2m4f. His only unplaced effort was when a close sixth in the Group 1 Grand Prix de Saint-Cloud over 1m4f, where he was not quite quick enough. There is every reason to believe he will be as good as ever this year, and he might even take his chance in the Ascot Gold Cup, now the drop back to middle-distances has proved unsuccessful. He can be expected to take a similar route to last year. ALAIN DE ROYER–DUPRE

VIA EGNATIA (USA)
3 b c Distorted Humor – Honest Lady (Seattle Slew)
Via Egnatia showed fair form in his first two starts as a 2yo over 6f at Yarmouth and Newbury, but on both occasions he pulled rather harder than ideal. However, once stepped up to a mile at Newmarket for this third outing and allowed to stride on, he looked a totally different horse, coming right away from an 82-rated rival with those in behind strung out like yesterday's washing. His pedigree has a big American influence –

he is a half-brother to a US Grade 1 winner out of a US Grade 1 winner – but he is also a half-brother to a couple of Listed winners on turf in Europe and his Newmarket performance shows that he is capable of smart form on grass. Expect to hear plenty more of him in 2017. JOHN GOSDEN

WALL OF FIRE (IRE)
4 b c Canford Cliffs – Bright Sapphire (Galileo)

It's fair to state Wall Of Fire has his own way of doing things. However, the son of Canford Cliffs took his form to a totally new level when tried as a stayer in the long-established Melrose Stakes at York's Dante meeting and he confirmed himself as going places when backing up in the Mallard – another top staying handicap – at Doncaster's St Leger meeting. His habit of dropping out early before rattling home strongly suggests there's very likely more in his locker and, versatile as regards going, it will be fascinating to chart how high he can climb in the Cup division as a 4yo. HUGO PALMER

WAR DECREE (USA)
3 b c War Front – Royal Decree (Street Cry)

War Front will soon have to shake off the impression that his progeny do not train on from two to three if he is to justify the enormous faith placed in him by Coolmore. After a few high-profile blowouts War Decree could be the horse to buck the trend. This lengthy, athletic colt ran only three times at two and connections can reap the rewards of that lighter campaign this season. Not yet the finished article when comfortably taking the 7f Group 2 Vintage Stakes at Glorious Goodwood, with Superlative Stakes conqueror Boynton back in third, natural progress ought to see him become a leading candidate for Europe's premier Classics over a mile. His relaxed manner through a race also brings races over 10f into the equation. AIDAN O'BRIEN

WESTWARD HO (IRE)
4 b g Fastnet Rock–Thought Is Free (Cadeaux Generereux)

Unraced at two, Westward Ho showed much-improved form to open his account at the third time of asking when taking a 1m maiden at Newcastle in October. Making ground on the bridle, he swept clear under hands-and-heels riding to score by two-and-a-half lengths. Raceform said: 'He looks the sort to win a nice handicap next year'. His long-established Middleham trainer sent out 15 winners from 146 runners in 2016 and this one will surely play his part in boosting the stable tally this time round. JAMES BETHELL

WINGS OF DESIRE
4 ch c Pivotal – Gull Wing (In The Wings)

Wings Of Desire achieved a great deal between a promising racecourse debut in the Wood Ditton at Newmarket in April and a lacklustre midfield finish in York's Juddmonte International Stakes at York in August. His highlights include success in the Dante, beating subsequent Group 1 winner Deauville, and a runners-up berth in the King George behind Highland Reel. In replicating his brother, Eagle Top, at Ascot he confirmed himself a colt of Group 1 calibre and, having been brought along slowly, significant progress can be expected as a four-year-old. Epsom's idiosyncrasies, rather than the softer ground, may have been his undoing when he was only fourth to Harzand in the Derby, which means that tailoring a campaign around races like the Hardwicke Stakes at Royal Ascot followed by another tilt at the King George could pay dividends. This muscular colt has the potential to surprise many. JOHN GOSDEN

WUHEIDA
3 ch f Dubawi – Hibaayeb (Singspiel)

The second foal of the Fillies' Mile, Ribblesdale and

Yellow Ribbon winner Hibaayeb, this daughter of Dubawi emulated her dam by taking a Group 1 as a juvenile. She won a 7f Newmarket maiden on her debut in August, with subsequent Group 3 winner Poet's Vanity back in fourth and then, on her only other start two months later, she took the Group 1 Prix Marcel Boussac. Ridden positively, she found plenty for pressure to wear down the long-time leader and score with a little in hand. The bare form leaves her with a little to find against the likes of Rhododendron, but she has a very good attitude and her breeding suggests that she might be more suited by middle-distances this season. On that basis the Oaks and similar contests might be right up her street. CHARLIE APPLEBY

YOU'RE HIRED
4 b c Dalakhani – Heaven Sent (Pivotal)
You're Hired won three of his four starts last year, notably Class 2 handicaps at Glorious Goodwood (despite racing wide) and at Yarmouth when last seen in September. His only defeat of the campaign came in a muddling contest at Goodwood which did not unfold to suit. You're Hired has had just six starts overall and is a well-bred colt who is expected to make the jump up to Group level this season. He will be suited by 1m4f. AMANDA PERRETT

YUCATAN (IRE)
3 b c Galileo – Six Perfections (Celtic Swing)
Yet to race beyond a mile in four starts at two, Yucatan is sure to step up in distance this season. Improving on his debut seventh at the Curragh, he ground out a victory over better-fancied stablemate Taj Mahal at the same venue three weeks later, before coping admirably with a jump into Group 2 company in the Beresford Stakes. Unable to handle the classier Capri, he was again seen to best effect once stamina

was at a premium, snatching second in the in the dying strides. He then deputised for that stablemate in Doncaster's Group 1 Racing Post Trophy, but he was outpaced as the race developed, which proved his undoing. Patently lacking the necessary gears required to trouble the winner, Rivet, this year's Derby may also be out of reach. Therefore, his connections could decide to make the most of his considerable assets at the earliest opportunity in the newly upgraded Group 2 Queen's Vase, a race they have won for the last two years with sons of Galileo. AIDAN O'BRIEN

ZOFFANIST (IRE)
3 ch g Zoffany – Frynia (Cat Thief)
Zoffanist ran modestly in three 7f-1m maidens last year, but that's reflected in an opening handicap mark of 64 and he should progress enough to win this year. He's a half-brother to a 10.5f Group 3 winner in France and can improve significantly when upped in trip. AMANDA PERRETT

INDEX TO HORSES

AKIHIRO (JPN)
ALGOMETER
ALMANZOR (FR)
ALPHA DELPHINI
AL WUKAIR (IRE)
ANDOK (IRE)
ANEEN (IRE)
ATTY PERSSE (IRE)

BEAN FEASA
BOYNTON (USA)
BRIAN THE SNAIL (IRE)
BRITTANIC (IRE)

CHAPKA (FR)
CHIPPING (IRE)
CLIFFS OF MOHER (IRE)
COLIBRI (IRE)
CORONET
CRACKSMAN
CRIMEAN TATAR (TUR)
CRYSTAL OCEAN

DABYAH (IRE)
DANCE KING
DHAJEEJ (IRE)
DOUBLE LADY (FR)
DREAMFIELD

EARTHA KITT
EASTON ANGEL (IRE)
ENABLE
EVERYTHING FOR YOU
  (IRE)

FAIR EVA
FAITHFUL CREEK (IRE)
FINAL VENTURE
FIRMAMENT
FLEETFOOT JACK (IRE)
FOREST RANGER (IRE)

GALIKEO
GARCIA
GIANT SPARK

GLITTER GIRL
GOLD LUCK (FR)

HARRY ANGEL (IRE)
HILARIO
HILARY J
HOLMESWOOD
HORSEPLAY

ICESPIRE
INCONCEIVABLE (IRE)
INTREPIDLY (USA)

JACK HOBBS
JOHANNES VERMEER (IRE)
JOSHUA REYNOLDS

KHAMAARY (IRE)
KHARBETATION (IRE)
KITTEN'S JOHNSTOWN
  (USA)
KRUGER PARK (IRE)

LEFT HAND
LIBRISA BREEZE
LIMATO (IRE)

MAKE TIME (IRE)
MAKKAAR (IRE)
MALMOOSA (IRE)
MONARCHS GLEN

NATIONAL DEFENSE

OMRAN
OUJA

PARLANCE (IRE)
PEALER (GER)
POET'S WORD (IRE)

QEMAH (IRE)
QUIET REFLECTION

REDICEAN
REMARKABLE

RIBCHESTER (IRE)
ROYAL ARTILLERY (USA)

SACRED ACT
SAINT EQUIANO
SCOONES
SENGA (USA)
SOFIA'S ROCK (FR)
SO MI DAR
STARGAZER (IRE)
STONE THE CROWS
SWISS STORM

TALAAYEB
TARTINI (USA)
THE TIN MAN
TIGERWOLF (IRE)
TRADING POINT (FR)

UAE KING
ULYSSES (IRE)

VAZIRABAD (FR)
VIA EGNATIA (USA)

WALL OF FIRE (IRE)
WAR DECREE (USA)
WESTWARD HO (IRE)
WINGS OF DESIRE
WUHEIDA

YOU'RE HIRED
YUCATAN (IRE)

ZOFFANIST (IRE)